17 REASONS
FOR
CYCLING FOR FUN AND FITNESS

A poll among 14,000 doctors during a Bicycle Health Week Campaign in England attested to the value of the bicycle and its effect upon every group of the population. Here are a few excerpts from the doctors' comments:

(1) "For people from 50 to 95, cycling keeps up elasticity of the blood vessels, prevents 'hard arteries' and high blood pressure so common in this age range. Cycling will be an insurance for preventing premature old age."

(2) "There can be no doubt that the general average of health among sedentary workers would be greatly improved if more use were made of the bicycle as a means of transport to and from work."

(3) "Useful for pleasure—with profit to health—useful for shopping. Keeps tissues 'oiled' and therefore benefits the circulation."

Dr. Paul Dudley White, noted American heart specialist, has written:

(4) "The establishment of cycling as a routine in the daily life of Americans, young and old, can become one of the most vital steps in restoring health and vigor to us all."

(5) "I'd like to put everybody on bicycles . . . Not once in a while, but regularly as a routine. That's a good way to prevent heart disease."

(6) "Bicycling is one of the best aids to physical fitness and health."

(7) "A rebirth of bicycling will bring health, economy, and pleasure."

(8) "Bicycling is an inexpensive routine of exercise that can be profitably enjoyed by every member of the family."

Dr. Irvine H. Page, president, American Heart Association:
(9) "We ought to replace the automobile with bicycles. . . . It would be better for our coronaries, our disposition, and certainly our finances."

Dr. W. W. Bauer, director emeritus, Bureau of Health Education, American Medical Association:
(10) "I think the bicycle is one of the great unappreciated vehicles for good, wholesome exercise that can be continued to a considerable age."

Former President Dwight D. Eisenhower:
(11) The nation's foremost sportsman has on several occasions advocated bicycle riding and gymnastics as a means of keeping young Americans physically fit. "America's children should ride their bikes more."

(12) The Dutch Public Health Congress published a documented report which disclosed that, two years after the introduction of the bicycle in school athletics and physical education in Holland, the number of sick school children dropped to 12 per cent. Particularly excellent results were noted in the reduction of sicknesses connected with growth and colds.

(13) Tests with similar results were cited in the Scandinavian countries. The health of Danish school children has appreciably improved. The famous Swedish gymnastics now include cycling, and school children from 12 to 20 years of age emerge from these courses more vigorous and more resistant to disease and disability.

(14) Professor Koelsch in Germany advises the bicycle for all those threatened by silicosis. It is well known that deep respiration has always been recommended for the prevention of this sickness, which is due to absorption of dust. The bicycle automatically compels the user to practice rhythmical, deep respiration. In the United States, Dr. Tabershom made the same observations as his German colleague in regard to the importance of the bicycle for treatment and prevention of silicosis. People with other respiratory afflictions also benefit by using the bicycle. According to specialists at several universities, the convalescence of tuberculosis patients is considerably accelerated by rational and supervised use of the bicycle.

(15) Medical care associations and the Health Protection Board in the United States have experimented with the use of the bicycle for treating bone diseases and have joined in recommending its use for children with weak bone structures.

(16) Premature aging can be delayed by the bicycle. The British Medical Board and the India Health and Welfare Protection Association affirmed this with supporting proof.

(17) Doctors now suggest to older people, when the heart and the circulatory system are satisfactory, to exercise on the bicycle in order to preserve a part of their youthful elasticity.

Cycling

By Roy Ald

FOREWORD by Paul Dudley White, M.D.,
with Curtis Mitchell

Grosset & Dunlap

A NATIONAL GENERAL COMPANY

PUBLISHERS   NEW YORK

The following organizations have been most co-operative with their guidance and the use of reference materials:

The Bicycle Institute of America
League of American Wheelmen
Amateur Bicycle League of America
Bicycle Touring League of America
American Youth Hostels, Inc.
Eastern Intercollegiate Cycling Association
Dr. Paul Dudley White's Committee for
   Safe Bicycling
American Institute of Park Executives, Inc.

All photographs courtesy of The Bicycle Institute of America.

ISBN: 0-448-00824-6

Library of Congress Catalog Card Number: 68-21294

Published simultaneously in Canada

Printed in the United States of America

A SPECIAL TRIBUTE TO
THE DISTINGUISHED CARDIOLOGIST
AND PRESIDENTIAL PHYSICIAN,
DR. PAUL DUDLEY WHITE

This one man, more than any other individual, has been the motivating force in the persuasion of more than 15 million American adults to participate in bicycling for their health, pleasure and physical fitness. As an influential advisor to a Congressional Conference on Bicycling in America, a national chairman of American Bike Month, president of the Committee for Safe Bicycling, Inc., writer of countless articles in both popular and professional journals, commending the life-giving benefits of this enjoyable activity, Dr. White has tirelessly carried his message forward to all Americans: "Get back on a bike." His influence accounts in no small measure for President Johnson's own pronouncement: "I see an America where bicycle paths, running through the hearts of our great cities, provide wholesome, healthy recreation for an entire family. . . ."

Dr. White, in his eighties, as an active cycling enthusiast, continues to serve as an inspirational example for his patients and millions of citizens everywhere. His contribution in terms of longer, happier, and more fulfilling lives for millions of active cyclists, of all ages, is inestimable. Long may he ride.

FOREWORD

by Paul Dudley White, M.D.
with Curtis Mitchell

Our soul is in our brain—a fact to which our clergy and psychiatrists should pay more attention. Our brain is nourished by our heart and our active muscles. Bicycles are an answer for both brain and body. If more of us rode them, we would have a sharp reduction in the use of tranquilizers and sleeping pills.

As a physician, I have recommended cycling to many patients as a way of keeping fit, provided their condition is suitable and provided they can cycle safely. And I advise cycling for healthy people to help keep them healthy.

In the first place, it is an aid to good muscle tone, much needed by the American people today. It aids the circulation, and thereby the heart and its work, by keeping the blood moving.

It aids the lungs through good tone of the diaphragm and makes it easier to bring oxygen into the body and pump out carbon dioxide.

It aids the nerves by improving sleep and maintaining equanimity and sanity.

It aids our digestion and it may even protect against peptic ulcers provided we don't try to establish a new speed record every day.

It aids our weight control if, at the same time, we keep the caloric and fat content of our diet where they belong.

It probably aids our longevity (like any other healthful exer-

9

cise) in reducing the amount of high blood pressure, coronary thrombosis, and diabetes which have engulfed us, although the certainty of this must be further determined by research.

And there are other benefits:

The bicycle costs little to own and operate. It can stand hard use. It requires no fuel. It can traverse all types of roads; if a road is blocked, the rider can walk and remount at the next clearing. Accidents are rare. And it saves acres of parking space, too.

Most important, I feel, is that the bicycle permits us to become acquainted again with the beauties of nature and with people. Though we get places fastest by airplane, it is a common experience that we see the least en route. But the bicycle, of all methods of transportation, gives us a chance to enjoy the countryside through which we ride and to meet its citizens.

AUTHOR'S NOTE

"Go ride a bike!" Certainly no exercise system has ever lured a physical fitness prospect with a more appealing invitation. In point of fact, that is all that the reader of *Cycling* is asked to do. The complete cycle exercise program has been devised to do the rest for him. Though it is simple to follow, much careful planning indeed has gone into the development of thoroughly enjoyable cycling schedules, tailormade for the individual according to his interest in cycling, his physical condition and his preferred cycling goal.

Whether eight, eighteen or eighty! Whether business executive, senior citizen, career girl, homemaker, collegian, city or country cousin, the pleasures and health benefits of cycling are present for the taking. If one hasn't been on a bike in years, or never at all, no matter. The gradual step-up cycling program is devised to meet him at the immediate level of his riding ability and move him rapidly up the scale of fitness and cycling proficiency.

For some, the goal may be an after-dinner "cycling constitutional" to release the day's tensions. For others, it may be weekend cycling trips or vacation tours, family riding or cycling club activities. Whatever the rider's goal, the Cycling Exercise Schedules designed for fitness Levels I (Standard), II (Intermediate) and III (Advanced) will firmly set him on the desired course. Their development came about when, as a physical instructor and operator of New York's Strength & Health Gymnasiums, the author measured the effects of the various physical fitness activities.

It was then he discovered that none could compare with the

all-around benefits of bicycling. Whether used in training professional athletes or as a therapeutic measure for recuperating invalids, its range and its applications seemed boundless at the same time that it proved itself to be the one prescription for regular and continuous exercise that people actually enjoyed following!

Cycling has been a romance of the author's for a quarter of a century and he feels confident that the reader will become equally enamored of it, through the practice of the "freewheeling" exercises outlined for him in the pages which follow.

CONTENTS

READER, PLEASE NOTE

Before you begin the Cycling for Fun and Fitness Exercises, or any other physical activity program, visit your doctor for a medical checkup. When you tell him what you have in mind, you and your doctor will probably end up cycling together!

CYCLING IS FUN—AND EXERCISE ISN'T

Most people in need of it are unhappily aware that the exercise road to physical fitness is paved with good intentions. When they cannot keep an exercise program going for very long, they assume that they are either lazy or have "weak will power." Not so!

In earlier times, the normal labors of daily living made enough physical demands on the body so that most people kept in shape by simply doing what came naturally. People did not have to think about resorting to the "daily dozen." Exercise— a word that had little meaning—was *built into their normal way of life*. But with the coming of modern mechanical devices, the body began to be deprived of the physical activity necessary for its health and well-being. Exercise now came into its own as something quite artificial, a kind of remedy which was to be tacked onto a normal day's activities in the form of calisthenic routines and body-building rituals.

Here we have the picture of exercise as an invented physical exertion which came to be regarded as a kind of necessary evil. Enter cycling—to save the day, and the reader's self-esteem! With the long list of medical benefits which qualify cycling as the *ideal* physical fitness activity, Dr. Paul Dudley White pointedly states: "First and foremost, riding a bicycle is *fun*." Secretary of the Interior Stewart L. Udall, himself an avid cyclist, seconds the motion for millions of riders when he says: "The bicycle is certainly unique when you recall how it is possible to combine so much health in the pursuit of pleasure."

THE EXERCISE SYSTEM THAT
ELIMINATES ITSELF

The clue to this enigma is the point we made about how people used to get their required amount of physical activity without ever thinking about exercise. That was before electric tooth-brushes, automatic can openers and remote control TV channel changers, of course. As we noted, their exercise was part of their normal living patterns.

This is what this book is really all about. Its cycling exercise schedules are designed to move the cycling activity, step by step, into *your* way of life. We defer again to Dr. White and more of his cogent words: "If bicycling can be fully restored *to the daily life* of all Americans, it can become a vital step toward rebuilding health and vigor in all of us." His address before the Congressional Conference on Bicycling in America clearly underscored this point of view. "I would like to put everybody on bicycles . . . not once in a while, but regularly as a routine. That is a good way to prevent heart disease." He went on to sum up this picture of cycling and cyclists by stating that their numbers are growing in leaps and bounds and that "their ages range from four to 84. They are riding tandems, unicycles, middleweights, touring bikes, adult three-wheelers, racers, and novelty bicycles of all kinds. . . . They ride for fun, health, sport and transportation. They ride under varying conditions and in every part of the countryside, to railroad stations, to shopping centers, to elementary and high schools, to and on college campuses, and they ride to their businesses and plants!" As you progress through *Cycling* you will discover that cycling has a place in your way of life in one or several forms.

16

Utilitarian

As a means of transportation, bikes are being used increasingly in vast government and defense installations, industrial plants, by executives and office workers and urban and suburban housewives. Dr. Irvine H. Page, former president of The American Heart Association, has affirmatively commented on this: "We ought to replace the automobile with the bicycle. . . . It would be better for our coronaries, our disposition, and certainly our finances." The automobile especially has become the target of many leading health authorities such as Harvard University's Dr. Jean Mayer, who implicates the car as a prime cause of the "absolutely miserable" physical shape and high incidence of heart disease in so many Americans. The confirmed cyclist soon discovers many advantages in "pedaling along" in instances where his bike can reasonably substitute for his automobile. And no gas bills or parking problems!

Recreation

Bicycling is for the fun of it—on outings, picnics, in family groups, as a "lone nomad on nature's trail," as a member of a bicycle club. The cycling exercise schedules prepare the rider for such activities and for more exciting recreational prospects: bicycling trips and tours, vacation travel here and abroad under conditions amenable to the interests and resources of the cyclist, financially and physically. *Cycling* will make the reader aware of all manner of bicycling facilities to accommodate the cycling enthusiast of any age and level of riding proficiency.

The graduating levels of the cycling exercise schedules lead the rider into the particular kind of cycling suitable to the individual's personal interests, abilities, and way of life. It is a physical fitness plan which keeps in mind at all times its ultimate objective: to eventually rid the reader of the onerous burden of exercise as drill and regimen. *It is from this point of view that cycling can be legitimately referred to as the exercise system that eliminates itself!*

DANGLE LOOSE AND RIDE EASY

Cycling is a get-out and get-with-it physical fitness book. As such, it recognizes the interest of the reader to perform rather than to sit and cogitate over medical data and details.

Relatively recent medical research findings, in pointing up the very real links between the lack of physical activity and the prevalent diseases of our time, have driven a great many people to exercise, almost any kind of exercise, out of anxiousness, even fear. This is a most unsatisfactory approach to exercise in view of the fact that the same medical research shows that hypertension is a serious complication of the leading high mortality diseases. Tension is the demon which our "exercise must exorcise" if it is to do us any good at all. Rushing headlong into *any* exercise regimen is evidently not the solution we seek. For example, the body building exercises relying upon isometric, weight-lifting and other muscular tension practices have serious limitations and are not for everyone. Undue attention to the outer frame muscles and their showy muscularity are not necessarily contributive to the internal health and vitality so critical for a life of prolonged activity and youthfulness.

For this, we must turn to the *circulatory exercises,* those physical movements which more fully activate the vital internal organs, the heart pump, the lungs, the diaphragm in absorbing and passing through greater quantities of the life-giving oxygen to stimulate blood circulation and re-energize the system. The exercise which best fulfills this requirement, at the same time that it is the most promising of adoption and continuance by millions of Americans of both sexes and all ages, is bicycling.

The ingredient which best accounts for this unique physical fitness phenomenon is the distinct sensation of relaxation which cycling encourages. The grace and coordination of the cycling motions, the natural rhythms which melt away hypertension will serve as a constant reminder of our message as you proceed from section to section of *Cycling*. Dangle loose and ride easy!

CYCLING FOR HEALTH
AND FITNESS

Cycling for Weight Control

Medical science has been learning a great many new things about the overweight condition, which has been called the No. 1 national health problem. Recent studies have shown how strategic is the factor of physical activity in the loss of excess body weight. At one time, the effect of exercise upon body weight was greatly minimized by all manner of rather insipid arguments such as: One would have to run up and down the Washington Monument so many times to burn up the calories in an extra pat of butter! Naturally, some exercises are a great deal more vigorous than others and do use up far more energy which can be expressed in terms of calories. Bicycling, for instance, is one of the more vigorous, and a cyclist can use up from 500 to 800 calories per hour.

Lately, medical science has proved that this simple calorie-counting approach was missing a strategic point: Regular and continuous circulatory exercises can "tilt the metabolic balance" and restore the body's automatic appetite control. This Apestat, as it is called, adjusts the appetite according to the individual's *actual* food need. In plain language, the only real hope of beating the overweight problem—not for several months, with this or that crash diet, but forever—is to combine an adequate amount of proper exercise with a sensible diet. Cycling is admirably suited to do the job!

A word or two about knowing whether you are overweight is also in order. Recent new medical information has shown that the usual weight scales according to body build do *not* tell the whole story. According to these scales, for example, one person might register as having a normal body weight and really be considerably more overweight than another who finds himself in the "fat" (20 pounds or more overweight) classification. To use an extreme example, the big fellow might be one of those strapping football players with great masses of solid muscle, while the tissues of the "normal" might be heavily laden with far too high a percentage of excess fat. The recent studies have demonstrated that body composition—the proportion of fat to muscle tissue—is the more critical measure of the overweight condition. The man or woman who takes little or no physical exercise but proudly lays claim to the same bodyweight at 50 as at 25, may even be carrying around enough fatty tissue to qualify as obese. Overall bodyweight may not have changed a single ounce, but how much of that bodyweight converted from solid tissue to flab, is quite another story!

Cycling for Figure Improvement

The individual inherits his or her bodily proportions and the tendency to put on weight in different places. Depending upon diet alone may take inches off where they cannot be spared and leave the trouble spots as shapeless as before. This is often the case in those most stubborn areas such as the ankles, legs and thighs, the buttocks and the waist, the underarms and the backs of the upper arms. A sustained program of cycling can go a long way toward remolding the figure to more pleasing proportions. There are few vigorous physical activities which lend themselves as ideally to the fitness objectives of both sexes—the ruggedly muscular male physique and the more graceful feminine contours. No difference in the exercises nor in the style of riding is recommended for either sex.

Cycling for Beauty

The grace and fluidity of the cycling motions promises those benefits most appealing to women, from the growing adolescent to the young-in-years mother or the young-in-heart grandmother.

A slimming shapeliness to limbs and waist, a radiant complexion and youthful skin enhanced by an enriched blood circulation, the look of alert, clear-eyed beauty are among cycling's more pronounced benefits for women.

Cycling for Health and Vitality

The daily accumulation of punishing nervous tensions are easily discharged with a pleasant, easy cycling glide, reducing the hazards of ulcers, high blood pressure, nagging insomnia. The real and psychological fatigue of boredom from household chores and highly specialized or sedentary jobs is quickly dispelled by a vigorous tune-up of the system and its vital organs. The generous oxygen supply to the brain for sharpened mental acuity accounts for Dr. White's remark that we can tell a great deal about a man's intelligence from the condition of his legs!

Cycling for Prolonged Youthfulness

The concentration of the physical action of cycling in the area of the pelvic girdle, with its vital organs and glands, is the special benefit to those in their middle and more advanced years. A firm toning of the muscles and an activated circulation and flexibility of the joints through continuous cycling holds out the promise of the youthful look and springy step of the 80-year-old gentleman cyclist who recently rode from New York to Los Angeles to visit his son!

ENTER YE OLDE BICYCLE

Now that we are only a tire toss away from the selection of the bike in your future, it might be interesting to take a swift backward glance at the bicycles of the past. This, and a few cogent points up to date, should instill a proper respect for the vehicle which has been referred to as "the father of the motorcar and grandfather of the airplane." It should also dispel the lingering notion that it is primarily a child's toy.

The wheel may well have been man's most remarkable invention, but it wasn't too much fun until 1816 when the Baron Karl von Drais assembled his Hobby Horse, as the first modern bicycle was called, and pushed himself along the street in Karlsruhe, Germany (he hadn't thought of pedals!). It was up to a wily Scotsman, Kirkpatrick MacMillan, likely out to save shoe leather, to come up with the idea for the pedals some twenty years later. For which painstaking inspiration he was unceremoniously ushered off the streets by the police for creating a public disturbance. The disturbance which greeted the velocipede, a version of the bicycle with two wooden wheels and iron tires which was introduced at the Paris Exposition in 1865, was of another sort—more to the life and limb of the rider of this "Boneshaker," as it was properly nicknamed, than to the public safety. To give the Boneshaker its due, however, it did become the ancestor to the modern safety bike.

The interest created in America by this vehicle was of a very special kind, attracting aviation pioneers Wilbur and Orville Wright and Glenn Curtis, as well as the automotive pioneers Henry Ford, Glenn Olds, George N. Pierce, among others. This vehicle played no minor role in the eventual development of the horseless carriage, that same automobile which Professor Mayer of Harvard blames as the main usurper of our physical activity today.

The bicycle models of our day, however, are a long way from the Hobby Horse and Boneshaker and all of the other eccentric and picturesque antique models in between. As an example, consider Jose Meiffret, the Frenchman who, on July 19, 1962, pedalled a bicycle at a speed clocked at 128 mph, the fastest that man has ever been able to travel under his own power. Of course, there are bicycle models suitable for the many cycling activities other than racing. Let us have a look at what is available for you to choose from for your rides for fun and fitness.

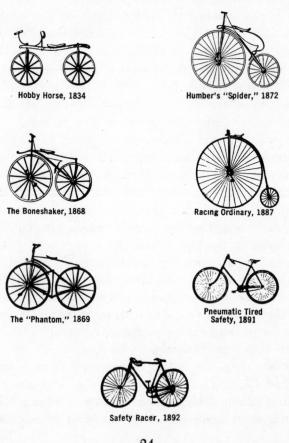

Hobby Horse, 1834

Humber's "Spider," 1872

The Boneshaker, 1868

Racing Ordinary, 1887

The "Phantom," 1869

Pneumatic Tired
Safety, 1891

Safety Racer, 1892

ON CHOOSING A BICYCLE

There is a bike for every riding season and reason, for everyone's pocketbook, in a sufficient variety of models to bedazzle novice and connoisseur alike.

There are many bike sizes, which, incidentally, are really a matter of wheel dimension these days, but the 26-inch size is for the adult. And that's that. The next step is almost as simple.

The two most popular styles are the American middleweight or utility bike, and the lightweight bike. Both are built for durability and easy, enjoyable riding and require minimum fuss and attention.

The Middleweight

This sturdy-framed model has picked up the reputation as an all-purpose bike over the years. It weighs about 45 to 50 pounds. If you intend to use your bike for convenient transportation as well as for community-area recreation riding, this model has its special virtues. For family rides, outings and picnics, when it's mighty handy to tote around some items for comfort and refreshment, the middleweight is capable of managing it well without interfering with the fun of the ride. Businessmen on the way to the office, communities of the "young retireds" turning to cycling, college campus riders, and cycling fitness fans intent upon hardy workouts often favor the middleweight stripped of all extraneous equipment.

The Lightweight

Weighing about 35 to 40 pounds, this is a more sophisticated model with hand brakes usually, and three speeds. It is easier for longer rides and over up-and-down terrain. The lighter weight and more versatile gear equipment eases the pedalling and accents the pleasure. The handling requires a bit more in the way of cycling skills and experience.

The Derailleur

This is a third basic type and it is even lighter than the lightweight. What's more, it has from five to 15 speeds! It works on a different gear system principle and it takes a top-level cyclist to get the most out of this bicycle. For long tours under come-what-may conditions, the Derailleur bike is the proper choice. It is frequently referred to as the touring bike. It is also the one used by bike racers, which suggests the high level competence called for in coaxing this high-strung model to yield its top-notch performance.

Gears Without Fears

More detail on the subject of gear handling is to be found under the heading "Up the Grade and Over the Hill" on page 78, but a few passing words are in order to take the mystery out of the subject. There is nothing formidable about the bicycle gearshift, as many inexperienced cyclists often assume.

In low gear, the rider happily discovers that it is a rare hill that he cannot pedal up-and-over with relative ease. What happens mechanically is that the gearshift allows the rider to take the hill in smaller, less laboring pedalling units. The three-speed lightweight is rapidly mastered. The Derailleur, with its five to 15 speeds, the bicycle of the "real pro," is as effective as the rider at the gears.

The Eccentrics

You have probably seen a rather eccentric-looking bike model around lately, and for the sake of touching all the bases, I hasten to include the type which is usually called the Compact or High-Riser. You know the one I mean because it has those real high handlebars and the cushiony banana seat mounted generally on a 20-inch frame. It is popular with the youngsters as a play bike because of its quick-turn advantage and it has its points for those interested in starting a bicycle drill team.

There are also other offbeat models catering to special cycling whims and interests. The One-Wheeled Unicycle and the Tandem bicycles built for two and more. The adult-size Tricycle is now coming into vogue with many senior citizens in retirement communities. There is a bold breed of antique cycle fanciers who may be seen blithely pedalling their turn-of-the-century "High Boys" along the thoroughfares to ogling eyes and craning necks!

WHERE DO I GO CYCLING?

Despite the fact that there is a bike boom all over the country and a rapid construction of bicycling facilities, if you have not given the subject any attention, you may very well ask this question. The listings under "Cycling Havens" on page 86 may give you a ready-made solution. If not, rest easy because there really isn't a problem. A little imagination in this respect can lead you to ideal cycling areas by the score. Here are a few off-the-cuff suggestions:

Check out playgrounds and parks and the sidewalks going alongside them. If you're fortunate enough to have a boardwalk, go off to a corner and quietly congratulate yourself. Then there often are concrete walks along the beach, lake shore perimeter paths, and promenades by the ocean.

Still not getting warm? Never fear. To borrow an expression from Jimmy Durante, "We've got a million of them!" How about bridle paths? Fairgrounds off-season? Abandoned railroad beds? Shopping-center parking areas after hours. Would you believe —parade grounds? If you live smack in the middle of a large city, look for those side streets, sidewalks, and streets headed for parks which are often designated for cycling. Even that tight little island of Manhattan has over 50 miles of bicycling paths! There are many cyclists who insist upon going their own way, nomad riders with the run of the community.

However you ride, be sure you ride safely and know the cycler's rules of the road. The safe-riding tips under the heading "Bikemanship" (page 75) will help prepare you for many years of happy, relaxed, hazard-free cycling for fun and fitness.

CLOTHES DO NOT A CYCLIST MAKE

What you wear to enjoy your bicycling activity is not too important so long as you dress comfortably and adequately according to the weather and do not favor garments that constrict the active blood circulation. Of course, what you are doing on a bicycle, where you are going, the time of day and your objective will dictate the general costume called for. You might be a housewife out to do some light shopping chores or to attend a PTA meeting. You could even be a public servant like Congressman Robert Eckhardt of Houston, pedalling to work on Capitol Hill. In these instances, we are not about to recommend shorts, jeans and sweatshirt. But adjustments in dress can be made to make cycling more pleasant, efficient and beneficial. The man in the business suit could loosen his collar and belt. If wearing a laced shoe, the tying should be secure but not too restricting on the foot. For the female cyclist, needless to say, *wear flats by all means.*

The shoes selected for cycling should be flexible and have enough give so that the shoe does not cause any uneven pressure and wearing against the foot from the continuous pedalling action. Cycling authority A. Fred DeLong recommends, in addition to cycling shoes, "Hush Puppies," low sneakers or bowling shoes for lightweight and nimble pedalling action. Footwear for cold weather should allow for the extra bulk of warmer socks.

For recreational and fitness cycling, jeans in denims of all kinds because of their sturdiness are quite popular, though one may find any old pair of pants or slacks adequate. If there is too much loose material in the pant leg, a bike clip is the wise precaution. For warm-weather cycling, shorts are excellent and a shirt with a loose, open collar. If you are light-skinned and pedalling under the bright sun, you should provide yourself with sufficient covering to avoid sunburn.

Exercise brings sweat, and a sweatshirt is a favored garment for all seasons. In colder weather, one can resort to an extra pullover which can be removed as he warms up to his activity. An important rule in general to apply to proper dress for cycling: Non-bulky lightweight clothing keeps in mind the fact that one warms up very rapidly from the vigorous exercise of cycling.

For all of this, the range of cycling fashion choice is too broad to be precisely categorized. The author has himself seen actor Anthony Perkins, an intrepid soul who favors the bicycle in midtown Manhattan traffic, pedalling over to a television studio, formally attired! And the Vogue-type models doing their rounds on wheels, in their stylish minis and maxis, breezing by the crush of taxis!

BACK ON A BIKE

Chances are that you have ridden a bike, but so far back that you don't even care to make a point of it. It doesn't matter, really, because we are going to proceed as if you hadn't. Most bicycle riders are self-taught and it is entirely possible that you may have picked up one or two bad habits which can be improved upon to make cycling that much more effortless and pleasurable for you. Those readers who are way past the few basics mentioned here can give them a glance and page by. Happily for the others, they will not be far behind because it is perfectly true that practically anybody can learn to ride a bike with a minimum of fuss and trial and error. A few expert tips will promptly have you pedalling down the road as if you were to the saddle born.

Trying on the Bike for Size

The correct-sized bike is an absolute must for a comfortable, untiring and well-controlled ride. Your local dealer can help you out on this score if you wish to buy one. If there is a nearby bike facility for rental and you wish to get the feel of a bike—trying one and another model before you buy—here are the points to look out for:

If the bike is too large you will have to stretch awkwardly to work the pedals and will unnecessarily exhaust yourself. If it is too small you will do the same by cramping your muscles, and it will also hamper your ability to steer. It isn't fun and it isn't safe. It is also unnecessary if you follow these checkpoints:

* The first thing to do is straddle the bike frame and see whether both feet comfortably and squarely meet the ground on either side.

* Next, in sitting upon the seat or saddle, turn the pedal down to "six o'clock," its bottom position, and see whether the heel of your foot rests on it. Is your leg fully extended, straight but not strained? Can you do the same with either leg without shifting in the saddle? If you can't, raise or lower the saddle accordingly.

* Once the saddle is adjusted, this calls for an adjustment in the handlebars. The rule is that the height of the saddle and the handlebar grips should be about the same.

* Make certain that the handlebars and seat are not raised so much that less than three inches of the handlebar stem and seat post are left imbedded in the bike frame.

Now that we have the matter of size attended to, let's get on with the next important step:

The Proper Riding Position

The rider's body is inclined forward, his arms extended before him on the handlebar grips so that his elbows, clear of his body, do not interfere with his steering. The saddle, level with the ground, can be adjusted forward or back for comfort and to ensure the fullest and most effective use of the legs and the body when pedalling. The forward-lean position makes this possible. Those who sit upright, backs straight, with all of their weight upon the saddle, will find their pedalling action hampered, inefficient, and rapidly fatiguing. For top performance and comfort, bicycling requires the coordinated use of the entire body. The upper torso, haunches, the muscles of the thighs, calves, the action of the ankles and the feet, should be brought into play. This not only places more power at the disposal of the rider, but insures that his effort is not exhaustingly concentrated at the thigh and the knee—a common fault, since it pre-

vents the all-important ankle joint from being brought into play, and drastically reduces pedalling proficiency. The rider should hasten to master the correct pedalling performance. The key is doing it right from the beginning before any long-lasting bad habits take over.

Pedalling Proficiency

First things first, and that refers to the position of the foot upon the pedal. Bad Habit No. 1 to strenuously avoid, or correct, is that of centering the instep upon the pedal and heavily pumping down. The secret of smooth and efficient pedalling lies in as complete a spin-around pedal action as possible. You must not be satisfied with the alternate pumpdown action. With lots of ankle action, you can help to carry the pedal back beyond its lowest position. In this way, you preserve the rhythmic, wholly

circular motion. Get the picture? To simplify it further, do not think "pedal *down*, pedal *down*" as you ride. Visualize instead, "pedal *around*, pedal *around*." After all, this is what cycling—from the word "cycle"—is all about.

Rider in the Balance

Getting on a bike for the novice, or getting *back* on a bike for the rider who has been off wheels for the proverbial dog's age, is primarily a matter of mastering the balancing act. It really is a snap, although it does not appear to be for the uninitiated. Keep up a steady forward momentum and the bike just naturally stands up on its own!

In any event, here is the easiest way to give yourself the assurance you need that you *can* balance yourself. The method is ideal for the novice and for the cyclist who wishes to test his steadiness on wheels after some years of inactivity.

I have found after many years of teaching cycling to people of all ages that the method of holding the seat from behind and running along behind the rider is *not* the most encouraging, and it often leads to a series of wobbling spills. Bike balance is better mastered by the rider without anyone's so-called assistance. He is able to move along in his own good time. The rider does not feel it necessary to prove his abilities too promptly for anyone else's benefit. Here's how it's done:

The seat is lowered so that the rider, when straddled upon it, can stand with both feet planted firmly on the ground. Now, taking hold of the handlebars, he begins pushing the bike along with his feet on the ground. This method is known as "scootering," and after five or ten minutes of it, the rider discovers that he can push and raise his feet, going several yards, balancing and steering all the time. Continuing in this way, the rider soon realizes that the bike, as long as it's kept moving, really balances itself and enables smooth and easy steering. If a gentle downgrade is somewhere nearby, so much the better for getting quickly past the scootering stage.

In using this method, I have taught youngsters in the five-to-seven age group, as well as a goodly number of senior citizens. I should modify my statement and say that I taught them, through scootering, *to teach themselves* how to ride a bike. Following the scootering stage, the raising of the seat to the proper position and the proper pedalling action are merely a step away.

A Pep Talk As You Move Closer to the Cycle Exercise Schedules

The first rule in cycling is to have fun. If you keep this in mind, then even the brush-up on your riding proficiency will be pursued in the spirit of "cycling games that people play." You will find that adopting or readopting the bicycle will be quite unlike any physical fitness regimen you may have previously tried and given up on. Cycling is no fad exercise that is approached with a hot enthusiasm that too rapidly cools. Bicycle riding stays with you and continues to grow on you, becoming more rewarding with the passing years. So, take it slow—you have a long way to go.

Sure as you are reading this page, cycling will rid you of all physical fitness problems and transform the chore to pleasure. Therefore, take the extra care and patience in the beginning to master the vehicle which offers you so many benefits. Practice mounting and dismounting, starting up and braking, taking curves and riding circles. And *before* you hit the road, make absolutely certain that you have thoroughly reviewed the Bikemanship section on page 75. Remember that every gain in riding skill and margin of safety will be a gain in your riding pleasure.

ON THE MARK—FOR THE CYCLE EXERCISE PROGRAM

Cycling exercise schedules have been developed for three levels with gradually increasing demands on physical fitness and riding skills. While each level serves as a distinct physical fitness unit, it is at the same time part of a comprehensive plan for stepping up the capacities of the rider. This permits him to approach the schedules without any other thought than to get out his bike and start rolling. In this way, he proceeds step by step and lets nature take its course.

The step-up method applies, as well, *within* each cycling exercise schedule. And through the expenditure of cycling effort, the rider distance covered and the cycling pace accelerated from levels I to III, they follow a somewhat similar pattern.

The cycling exercises have been fashioned for *body toning, body conditioning,* and *body development,* and they are introduced into each cycling session in this order: There is a *warm-up cycle,* a *training cycle,* and a *bike run.*

Level I includes, as well, a special set of riding exercises: *Cyclesthenics—*"calisthenics for the cyclist" on his way to cycling fitness. Cyclesthenics helps him to release muscle tension, build up breathing capacity, strengthen the lower back, the abdomen and the leg muscles. *Cyclesthenics are designed to give the novice or the poorly conditioned rider a head start on his way to cycling fitness.*

While a special feature of the level I cycle exercise schedules, cyclesthenics play a more limited part as the rider progresses. Presently, the happy habit of regular and vigorous cycling takes over and naturally fulfills all physical fitness needs without any thought of them whatever! This objective of the cycling exercise program becomes obvious when the rider discovers that the cycle exercise level leads him *beyond* scheduled riding drills into cycling activities which suit his interests and way of life.

The cycling exercise schedules which lead to this agreeable prospect are enjoyable and highly exhilarating rides. Unlike any other exercise forms, cycling has no constant stop-and-go and awkward shifts to new exercises. *The cyclist takes each exercise session in one continuous ride.* Even his "rests" are taken while pleasantly coasting along, a practice which is described in the exercise schedules as a "coastaway."

THE TIME FOR FITNESS

The cycling exercises require very little time, really. Even the most demanding cycling session, which comes at the sixth week of levels I, II and III, requires no more than 30 minutes. With two cycle exercise sessions each week, a scheduled "joyride" and a longer weekend pleasure ride, the cyclist will find it to be a most undemanding time schedule. Though as the reader knows, time itself has that peculiar quality of somehow being more available for those things which are the most enjoyed than for those tasks which *should* be done.

This is not so much a human fault as it is a natural condition of our lives. Those activities which are a part of the daily routine are performed almost automatically. Those, like physical exercise, which we must find the time to replace in our lives, are somehow put off. So we are back again to that wonderful advantage of cycling activity. It *can* become part of our way of life.

The cycle exercise program encourages this by allowing the cyclist to include his general riding mileage as part of the weekly totals required by the schedules.

There is a hitch to this, however. The cyclist must complete at least the nine weeks of schedule I, up to the full competency level required before he or she is qualified to deduct general riding time from the standard cycling exercise schedules.

The cycling exercise schedules may then be used by the cyclist to build himself up to more demanding levels of cycling fitness and proficiency.

SOME WAYS TO KEEP TRACK OF DISTANCE

The cycle exercise schedules are planned to make keeping track of distance easy. Each cycle exercise level does have its own time-mileage goal, but much of this has been built into the exercises so that the rider need not give any thought to it. He concentrates instead on counting off, *rhythmically*, so many pedal-turns (PTs) as he rolls along. Bicycle exercises require more effort than normal casual riding. This energy measure is used to build up the cyclist's fitness for the longer rides of higher levels. By performing these exercises as described, the rider is automatically carrying himself forward to the prescribed goal. (But there is even more importance in the PT counting system, as the reader will presently discover in the next section!)

Where actual distances are called for during the cycling sessions or "workouts," they are noted in handily divisible parts of a mile—¼, ½ and so on. With a bit of imagination, the rider will discover many ways of managing this without a concern for "yard-splitting." He may be sufficiently familiar with an area and generally know the distances from one point to another. He may figure out and settle on certain landmarks. Taking a few turns in a car with an eye on the odometer can help mark off a course. Or the "city block" formula can be used.

Of course, soon enough, the cycling enthusiast hastens to acquire the inexpensive cyclometer, the mileage meter which is a snap to put on his bicycle. He becomes interested in knowing just how many miles he is accumulating under his own foot-power. Whether shopping, clubbing, weekending out, on bike vacations or cycling to work, every mile is all honest grist for the cyclist's mileage mill! As common and as prideful as the fisherman's "It was this big . . ." is the cyclist's opening conversational thrust—"Know how many miles I did last (weekend, week, month or year)?" But remember—at least the full nine weeks of level I must be completed before the cyclist qualifies.

For this reason, there is no immediate need for any mileage meter. As a matter of fact, the reader is urged *not* to consider it until he or she has, at the very least, reached the qualifying cycle exercise goal. By then, many riders, "back on a bike" to stay, may consider their personal cycling goals as already fulfilled. They will be well on their way to cycling for fun and fitness, whether or not they wish to play the avid cyclist's mileage game.

PTs AND THE NATURAL BODY RHYTHMS

"I've Got Rhythm" is the ideal cyclist theme song, and the next line, "Who could ask for anything more?" is just as applicable.

If there is any quality to be singled out for the rider to concentrate on, especially in the beginning, it would have to be the smooth regularity of the pedalling rhythms. In this lies the key to skillful and pleasurable cycling as well as to extremely important physical fitness and health benefits.

The physician uses the body's natural bio-rhythms as indicators of physical well being. The pulsebeat, the heartbeat rhythms, the rhythm of the brain waves, the metabolic rhythms. Rhythms which are too speeded up or too sluggish affect not only organ function but psychological attitude. On a day when the bio-rhythms are "irregular," one feels out of sorts and *not with it*. There is a notable lack of coordination. Chores are performed less efficiently. Interestingly, the body registers pain itself as a disordered body rhythm.

Cycling, especially properly *rhythmic* cycling, can contribute much to restoring and maintaining normal biorhythms.

The pedal-turn (PT) counting system has been especially devised to help the cyclist concentrate his attention on his foot pedalling and the rhythms of the ride. With higher pedalling proficiency, such rhythms soon become unconscious habit for the good cyclist. For this reason, the PT count is eventually dropped. It does not appear at all in level III. If by then, rhythmic pedalling is not mastered as part of the rider's "second nature," these advanced cycling exercise schedules are not for him.

Rhythmic cycling means more pleasant and enjoyable riding

—getting the most out of the least effort. The proficient cyclist attends to his pedalling rhythms and not his cycling speed. So to help get the knack of it—especially in the beginning—watch your PTs. And remember that one good turn deserves another!

LEVEL I IS FOR YOU—IF

. . . you have definitely been the sedentary type. Using your car and your remote control TV channel changer instead of your feet . . .

. . . you carry around the merit of extra years and *have taken things easy* because *other* people think it's the thing for someone "that age" to do . . .

. . . you are active in some activity which uses a limited part of your body and your capacities . . .

. . . you suffer from psychological fatigue and drowsiness and find it an effort to get up and do things or go places . . .

. . . you are all wound up, under high pressure, sit on the edge of chairs and are an incessant hand or foot tapper . . .

. . . you are overweight, say twenty pounds or more, and you *know* it isn't muscle tissue . . .

. . . you smoke too much and become short-winded from mild activity . . .

. . . you want to engage in healthful and vigorous exercise but just as little as you need of it to keep in reasonably good shape . . .

. . . you *are* athletically inclined but bicycling is not something you ever got around to do, or haven't done for a long time.

BICYCLE EXERCISE SCHEDULES
ARE SELF-PROGRESSIVE

You don't lose a thing by beginning at the beginning, because you move ahead quickly according to your own increasing capability. Perhaps you needed only to get the hang of it, develop some bikemanship, or limber up muscles you haven't used before or for quite some time. Fine, move on up—the way is open if the will and the capability is there. However, *do* take full advantage of the system of step-up physical conditioning and trust in the performance of your own body as you cycle. It is the best indicator of how fast you should move up.

You should not feel over-taxed and over-exhausted as a result of your cycling sessions. Expended, yes, but pleasantly so—sleeping better and waking up more alert because of the exhilarating cycling exercises.

Chances are that you will move along easily in the beginning (if you don't, your physical condition or bikemanship does not warrant it) and will presently arrive at a level where the workouts become more challenging. As soon as you do, respect the schedules and stay with them until you feel the beginning of a new physical breakthrough. You will know it when it comes. The hard part no longer seems so hard, and what tired you before does so no longer.

ACHES AND PAINS

Aches and pains are a normal part of any vigorous exercise. Especially in the beginning as new sets of muscles face their baptism under fire. Also, as you approach new and higher plateaus of development. The aches and pains which should be disturbing are those which accompany *in*activity. This is a sign of poor muscle tone, sluggish circulation, and stiffening joints. In a word, aging. And in our physically inactive way of life, it can begin even at age twenty-five!

The aches and pains from vigorous exercise are signs that the body is throwing off decrepitude and girding itself for more challenging demands. They pass quickly enough and may be slowly worked out with gradual, easy cycling. If you need a few days of rest for aching calves or thighs, no one is going to take back your merit badge! Keep in mind the happy cycling for fun and fitness slogan—"Dangle loose and ride easy."

THE CYCLESTHENIC WAY

The fascinating thing about these "calisthenics on a cycle" is this: As you master them, they begin to disappear from your cycling exercise schedules. They are wonderful for stretching and limbering the body. Performed as you pedal along, they give you that extra nudge up the cycling fitness ladder—until you can manage very well under your own cycling steam, thank you!

Actually, they require no special instruction. They can be performed at a glance, with the illustrations given on the next two pages—and their descriptive names—to guide you. But to understand what they help you accomplish, you may wish to read through the following:

The Dangle:

This is a reminder of the message, "Dangle loose and ride easy." It is the posture used for the *warmup ride* which is the first of each cycle exercise session. To "dangle"—*ease up.* Let your body slump a bit. Let your head hang easy on your neck. Your shoulders drop. Looser. More flex in wrist, knee and ankle joints. There, you have it! Now all you have to do is pedal and glide away, keeping time to the easy rhythm of the wheels. The dangle is *the warmup* for what is to follow. Next for the tune-up.

The Breather:

If a Martian were to describe an Earthman (or his better half), he would likely refer to him as bellows, an air inhalation and exhalation machine. As long as he didn't say "a bag of wind," he wouldn't be far wrong.

Let us help along those vital "pump organs," heart and lungs,

to provide us with a richer supply of life-giving oxygen and "release of the carbon dioxide wastes." The breather will put you in a frame of mind to emphasize this rich benefit of bicycling —and to suck in that air!

You do the breather as you should by combining a quick succession of pedal turns with deep inhalations of air. Pedal—gulp (hold it!). Pedal—gulp more. Another pedal and gulp on top of that until you're full up. Then—as you go into a coastaway, let go! Flush out those lungs. You will be amazed to discover how much regular cycling will help to enlarge the vital, lifegiving capacity of your air intake.

The West Point:

Attention, forward ride! might be the signal for this one. Ramrod stiff—chest way out, and butt the same. Swaybacked as a scared plebe. We want to get at those important muscles in the small of the back. Now, stand and ride as if doing a marching step.

The Racer:

Bring the upper torso forward, hunching up your back, racerstyle. This is often called a "C body position." Visualize a grey-

hound in flight, because an important detail in this one is to
pull in your tummy, at least as far in as you can—and hold it
there as you pedal away.

Let's restore the muscles of the stomach, which should be a
kind of retaining wall, a defense for your vital organs.

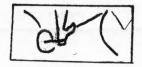

The Heelaway:

This one calls for putting the pedalling effort as far back on
the heel of the foot as possible. No, this is *not* an approved
pedalling style. but we want to get to unused or little-used
tendons and joints. You have to feel this one in the ankle joint
and in back of the knee and thigh as your foot "heels the pedals."

The Toedown:

This time, you pedal with the way-up-front part of your foot,
depending as much as possible upon the toes only. Do as well
as you can. You will improve quickly and so will those muscles
and "oiled up" joints you need for efficient fun-and-fitness
cycling.

LEVEL I: THE STANDARD CYCLING EXERCISE SCHEDULES

* Points of focus: to get the reader "back on a bike" and bring him up to standard fitness and cycling proficiency.

* The standard exercise schedules reach a 25-mile weekly riding peak. Achievement of this goal equips the cyclist for the range of recreational activities under "cycling day trips."

* A slow/moderate cycling pace will keep the rider within the recommended 7–10 mph range in doing level I cycling exercises.

* Special care should be exercised by level I riders in the selection of cycling routes. Smooth, firm riding surfaces are best. Keep to level ground. For further instructions on this subject, refer to "Up the Grade and Over the Hill," page 78.

DEFINITIONS

PTs—Pedal Turns. The cycle exercise count, the equivalent of "Hup-two-three-four!" Continuous rhythmic pedal turns to the required number indicated in the schedule.

Coastaway—The coasting to ease up after PT count.

Recovery Coastaway—The longer coasting following set of cycling exercises.

On Saddle—Pedaling while seated.

Off Saddle—Pedaling from standing position.

Joyride—Relax and go! Strictly a freestyle ride. If it's *optional*, take it or leave it. If it's *scheduled*, you gotta go!

HOW IT'S DONE

1. WARMUP CYCLE. This is the tension breaker.

2. CYCLESTHENICS. These are for limbering up. (See pages 47–49 for descriptions.)

3. TRAINING CYCLE. This is the step-up cycling conditioner.

4. TEST RUN. The developer and progressive improvement guage.

5. THE WEEKEND WORKOUT. The leisure ride. It's great fun and you reap the benefits of the graduated cycling program. The miles melt away under easy, rhythmic pedalling.

WEEK ONE

Slow/Moderate
(7–10 MPH)

(See page 51, "How
It's Done")

MONDAY
Standard Cycling Exercises

1. Warmup Cycle:	"Dangle loose, ride easy."	Distance: ⅛ mile	
2. Cyclesthenics:	The Breather	Count: 6 PTs	
		Coastaway	
	The West Point	Count: 6 PTs	
		Coastaway	
	The Racer	Count: 6 PTs	
		Coastaway	
	The Heelaway	Count: 6 PTs	
		Coastaway	
	The Toedown	Count: 6 PTs	
		Recovery Coastaway	
3. Training Cycle:	On Saddle	Count: 10 PTs	
		Coastaway	
	On Saddle	Count: 10 PTs	
		Recovery Coastaway	
	REPEAT SEQUENCE:	4 TIMES	
4. Test Run:	On Saddle	Distance: ½ mile	

TUESDAY Rest or optional "joyride" Distance: ¾ mile

WEDNESDAY
Standard Cycling Exercises

1. Warmup Cycle:	"Dangle loose, ride easy."	Distance: ⅛ mile	
2. Cyclesthenics:	[Same as above].		
3. Training Cycle:	On Saddle	Count: 10 PTs	
		Coastaway	
	Off Saddle	Count: 10 PTs	
		Recovery Coastaway	
	REPEAT SEQUENCE:	3 TIMES	
4. Test Run:	On Saddle	Distance: ½ mile	

THURSDAY Scheduled "joyride" Distance: 1 mile

FRIDAY Rest Day

**WEEKEND
WORKOUT** Leisure Ride. Stop and go
as you choose. (At least
2 miles non-stop.) Distance: 5 miles

MONDAY
Standard Cycling Exercises

1. Warmup Cycle:	"Dangle loose, ride easy."	Distance: ⅛ mile	
2. Cyclesthenics:	The Breather	Count: 6 PTs Coastaway	
	The West Point	Count: 6 PTs Coastaway	
	The Racer	Count: 6 PTs Coastaway	
	The Heelaway	Count: 6 PTs Coastaway	
	The Toedown	Count: 6 PTs Recovery Coastaway	
	REPEAT SEQUENCE:	2 TIMES	
3. Training Cycle:	Off Saddle	Count: 10 PTs Coastaway	
	Off Saddle	Count: 10 PTs Recovery Coastaway	
	REPEAT SEQUENCE:	3 TIMES	
4. Test Run:	On and Off Saddle	Distance: ½ mile	

TUESDAY   Rest or optional "joyride"   Distance: 1 mile

WEDNESDAY
Standard Cycling Exercises

1. Warmup Cycle:	"Dangle loose, ride easy."	Distance: ⅛ mile	
2. Cyclesthenics:	[Same as above].		
3. Training Cycle:	On Saddle	Count: 15 PTs Coastaway	
	On Saddle	Count: 15 PTs Recovery Coastaway	
	REPEAT SEQUENCE:	4 TIMES	
4. Test Run:	On Saddle	Distance: ¾ mile	

THURSDAY   Scheduled "joyride"   Distance: 1½ miles

FRIDAY   Rest Day

WEEKEND WORKOUT   Leisure Ride. Stop and go as you choose. (At least 3 miles non-stop.)   Distance: 8 miles

MONDAY
Standard Cycling Exercises

1. Warmup Cycle:	"Dangle loose, ride easy."	Distance: ¼ mile
2. Cyclesthenics:	The Breather	Count: 8 PTs Coastaway
	The West Point	Count: 8 PTs Coastaway
	The Racer	Count: 8 PTs Coastaway
	The Heelaway	Count: 8 PTs Coastaway
	The Toedown	Count: 8 PTs Recovery Coastaway
3. Training Cycle:	On Saddle	Count: 15 PTs Coastaway
	Off Saddle	Count: 15 PTs Recovery Coastaway
	REPEAT SEQUENCE:	3 TIMES
4. Test Run:	On Saddle	Distance: ¾ mile

TUESDAY   Rest or optional "joyride"   Distance: 1 mile

WEDNESDAY
Standard Cycling Exercises

1. Warmup Cycle:	"Dangle loose, ride easy."	Distance: ¼ mile
2. Cyclesthenics:	[Same as above].	
3. Training Cycle:	Off Saddle	Count: 15 PTs Coastaway
	Off Saddle	Count: 15 PTs Recovery Coastaway
	REPEAT SEQUENCE:	3 TIMES
4. Test Run:	On and Off Saddle	Distance: ¾ mile

THURSDAY   Scheduled "joyride"   Distance: 1½ miles

FRIDAY   Rest Day

WEEKEND WORKOUT   Leisure Ride. Stop and go as you choose. (At least 4 miles non-stop.)   Distance: 10 miles

| LEVEL I | **WEEK FOUR** | Slow/Moderate (7–10 MPH) |

MONDAY
Standard Cycling Exercises

1. Warmup Cycle:	"Dangle loose, ride easy."	Distance: ¼ mile
2. Cyclesthenics:	The Breather	Count: 8 PTs Coastaway
	The West Point	Count: 8 PTs Coastaway
	The Racer	Count: 8 PTs Coastaway
	The Heelaway	Count: 8 PTs Coastaway
	The Toedown	Count: 8 PTs Recovery Coastaway
	REPEAT SEQUENCE:	2 TIMES
3. Training Cycle:	On Saddle	Count: 20 PTs Coastaway
	On Saddle	Count: 20 PTs Recovery Coastaway
	REPEAT SEQUENCE:	4 TIMES
4. Test Run:	On Saddle	Distance: 1 mile
TUESDAY	Rest or optional "joyride"	Distance: 1½ miles

WEDNESDAY
Standard Cycling Exercises

1. Warmup Cycle:	"Dangle loose, ride easy."	Distance: ¼ mile
2. Cyclesthenics:	[Same as above].	
3. Training Cycle:	On Saddle	Count: 20 PTs Coastaway
	Off Saddle	Count: 20 PTs Recovery Coastaway
	REPEAT SEQUENCE:	3 TIMES
4. Test Run:	On and Off Saddle	Distance: 1 mile
THURSDAY	Scheduled "joyride"	Distance: 2 miles
FRIDAY	Rest Day	
WEEKEND WORKOUT	Leisure Ride. Stop and go as you choose. (At least 5 miles non-stop.)	Distance: 10 miles

MONDAY
Standard Cycling Exercises
  1. Warmup Cycle: "Dangle loose, ride easy." Distance: ½ mile
  2. Cyclesthenics: The Breather Count: 10 PTs
  Coastaway

  The West Point Count: 10 PTs
  Coastaway

  The Racer Count: 10 PTs
  Coastaway

  The Heelaway Count: 10 PTs
  Coastaway

  The Toedown Count: 10 PTs
  Recovery Coastaway
  3. Training Cycle: Off Saddle Count: 20 PTs
  Coastaway

  Off Saddle Count: 20 PTs
  Recovery Coastaway
  REPEAT SEQUENCE: 3 TIMES
  4. Test Run: On and Off Saddle Distance: 1 mile

TUESDAY Rest or optional "joyride" Distance: 1½ miles

WEDNESDAY
Standard Cycling Exercises
  1. Warmup Cycle: "Dangle loose, ride easy." Distance: ½ mile
  2. Cyclesthenics: [Same as above].
  3. Training Cycle: On Saddle Count: 25 PTs
  Coastaway

  On Saddle Count: 25 PTs
  Recovery Coastaway
  REPEAT SEQUENCE: 4 TIMES
  4. Test Run: On Saddle Distance: 1½ miles

THURSDAY Scheduled "joyride" Distance: 2 miles

FRIDAY Rest Day

**WEEKEND
  WORKOUT** Leisure Ride. Stop and go
  as you choose. (At least
  7 miles non-stop.) Distance: 15 miles

WEEK SIX

MONDAY
Standard Cycling Exercises

1. Warmup Cycle:	"Dangle loose, ride easy."	Distance: ½ mile
2. Cyclesthenics:	The Breather	Count: 10 PTs
		Coastaway
	The West Point	Count: 10 PTs
		Coastaway
	The Racer	Count: 10 PTs
		Coastaway
	The Heelaway	Count: 10 PTs
		Coastaway
	The Toedown	Count: 10 PTs
		Recovery Coastaway
	REPEAT SEQUENCE:	2 TIMES
3. Training Cycle:	On Saddle	Count: 25 PTs
		Coastaway
	Off Saddle	Count: 25 PTs
		Recovery Coastaway
	REPEAT SEQUENCE:	3 TIMES
4. Test Run:	On Saddle	Distance: 1½ miles

TUESDAY	Rest or optional "joyride"	Distance: 2 miles

WEDNESDAY
Standard Cycling Exercises

1. Warmup Cycle:	"Dangle loose, ride easy."	Distance: ½ mile
2. Cyclesthenics:	[Same as above].	
3. Training Cycle:	Off Saddle	Count: 25 PTs
		Coastaway
	Off Saddle	Count: 25 PTs
		Recovery Coastaway
	REPEAT SEQUENCE:	3 TIMES
4. Test Run:	On and Off Saddle	Distance: 1½ miles

THURSDAY	Scheduled "joyride"	Distance: 3 miles
FRIDAY	Rest Day	
WEEKEND WORKOUT	Leisure Ride. Stop and go as you choose. (At least 8 miles non-stop.)	Distance: 15 miles

WHERE DO YOU GO FROM HERE?

The cycle exercise schedule for week six—level I—*is to be continued for three additional weeks*, at which time its goals will have been attained IF:

(1) The rider's cycling pace peaks at 10 mph for the various exercise activities.

(2) The workout period for week six exercise schedule does not exceed 30 minutes.

(3) The weekend ride of 15 miles can be accomplished non-stop.

(4) The rider's weekly cycling mileage total is not less than 25 miles.

At this level of accomplishment, the rider is considered capable of cycling day trips and outings, page 81.

He or she may decide to maintain this level of proficiency with less formal cycling practice or a continuance of level I cycle exercise schedules. Since the ninth week level has been reached, the rider can now begin to include any cycling activities—utilitarian, recreational and/or cycling exercise—in the total weekly riding mileage.

Those with an interest in raising their fitness and bicycling proficiency higher may proceed to level II, intermediate cycle exercise schedules.

LEVEL II: THE INTERMEDIATE CYCLING EXERCISE SCHEDULES

* Points of focus: the above-average fitness, coordination and physical reserves of the intermediate-level cyclist.

* The intermediate exercise schedules attain a 50-mile weekly riding peak. This accomplishment qualifies the cyclist for the range of recreational activities under tourism on a bike and as a member of cycling clubs.

* A medium cycling pace will keep the rider within the 12–15 mph range recommended in the performance of level II cycling exercises.

* The intermediate rider is prepared for a more versatile cycling terrain. Reference should be made to level II, "Up the Grade and Over the Hill," page 78.

(See page 51, "How
It's Done")

MONDAY
Intermediate Cycling Exercises

1. Warmup Cycle:	"Dangle loose, ride easy."	Distance: ¾ mile
2. Cyclesthenics:	The Breather	Count: 10 PTs Coastaway
	The Racer	Count: 10 PTs Recovery Coastaway
3. Training Cycle:	On Saddle	Count: 30 PTs Coastaway
	On Saddle	Count: 30 PTs Recovery Coastaway
	REPEAT SEQUENCE:	4 TIMES
4. Test Run:	On and Off Saddle	Distance: 2 miles

TUESDAY	Rest or optional "joyride"	Distance: 2¼ miles

WEDNESDAY
Intermediate Cycling Exercises

1. Warmup Cycle:	"Dangle loose, ride easy."	Distance: ¾ mile
2. Cyclesthenics:	[Same as above].	
3. Training Cycle:	On Saddle	Count: 30 PTs Coastaway
	Off Saddle	Count: 30 PTs Recovery Coastaway
	REPEAT SEQUENCE:	3 TIMES
4. Test Run:	On and Off Saddle	Distance: 2 miles

THURSDAY	Scheduled "joyride"	Distance: 2½ miles
FRIDAY	Rest Day	
WEEKEND WORKOUT	Leisure Ride. (At least 10 miles non-stop.)	Distance: 20 miles

MONDAY
Intermediate Cycling Exercises

1. Warmup Cycle:	"Dangle loose, ride easy."	Distance: ¾ mile
2. Cyclesthenics:	The Breather	Count: 10 PTs
		Coastaway
	The Racer	Count: 10 PTs
		Recovery Coastaway
	REPEAT SEQUENCE:	2 TIMES
3. Training Cycle:	Off Saddle	Count: 30 PTs
		Coastaway
	Off Saddle	Count: 30 PTs
		Recovery Coastaway
	REPEAT SEQUENCE:	3 TIMES
4. Test Run:	On & Off Saddle	Distance: 2 miles
TUESDAY	Rest or optional "joyride"	Distance: 2½ miles

WEDNESDAY
Intermediate Cycling Exercises

1. Warmup Cycle:	"Dangle loose, ride easy."	Distance: ¾ mile
2. Cyclesthenics:	[Same as above].	
3. Training Cycle:	On Saddle	Count: 35 PTs
		Coastaway
	On Saddle	Count: 35 PTs
		Recovery Coastaway
	REPEAT SEQUENCE:	4 TIMES
4. Test Run:	On and Off Saddle	Distance: 2¼ miles
THURSDAY	Scheduled "joyride"	Distance: 3 miles
FRIDAY	Rest Day	
WEEKEND WORKOUT	Leisure Ride. (At least 12 miles non-stop.)	Distance: 23 miles

MONDAY
Intermediate Cycling Exercises

1. Warmup Cycle:	"Dangle loose, ride easy."	Distance: 1 mile
2. Cyclesthenics:	The Breather	Count: 15 PTs Coastaway
	The Racer	Count: 15 PTs Recovery Coastaway
3. Training Cycle:	On Saddle	Count: 35 PTs Coastaway
	Off Saddle	Count: 35 PTs Recovery Coastaway
	REPEAT SEQUENCE:	3 TIMES
4. Test Run:	On and Off Saddle	Distance: 2¼ miles

TUESDAY	Rest or optional "joyride"	Distance: 3 miles

WEDNESDAY
Intermediate Cycling Exercises

1. Warmup Cycle:	"Dangle loose, ride easy."	Distance: 1 mile
2. Cyclesthenics:	[Same as above].	
3. Training Cycle:	Off Saddle	Count: 35 PTs Coastaway
	Off Saddle	Count: 35 PTs Recovery Coastaway
	REPEAT SEQUENCE:	3 TIMES
4. Test Run:	On and Off Saddle	Distance: 2¼ miles

THURSDAY	Scheduled "joyride"	Distance: 3½ miles
FRIDAY	Rest Day	
WEEKEND WORKOUT	Leisure Ride. (At least 15 miles non-stop.)	Distance: 25 miles

MONDAY
Intermediate Cycling Exercises
1. Warmup Cycle:	"Dangle loose, ride easy."	Distance: 1 mile
2. Cyclesthenics:	The Breather	Count: 15 PTs
		Coastaway
	The Racer	Count: 15 PTs
		Recovery Coastaway
	REPEAT SEQUENCE:	2 TIMES
3. Training Cycle:	On Saddle	Count: 40 PTs
		Coastaway
	On Saddle	Count: 40 PTs
		Recovery Coastaway
	REPEAT SEQUENCE:	4 TIMES
4. Test Run:	On and Off Saddle	Distance: 2½ miles

TUESDAY	Rest or optional "joyride"	Distance: 3½ miles

WEDNESDAY
Intermediate Cycling Exercises
1. Warmup Cycle:	"Dangle loose, ride easy."	Distance: 1 mile
2. Cyclesthenics:	The Breather	Count: 20 PTs
		Coastaway
	The Racer	Count: 20 PTs
		Recovery Coastaway
3. Training Cycle:	On Saddle	Count: 40 PTs
		Coastaway
	Off Saddle	Count: 40 PTs
		Recovery Coastaway
	REPEAT SEQUENCE:	3 TIMES
4. Test Run:	On and Off Saddle	Distance: 2½ miles

THURSDAY	Scheduled "joyride"	Distance: 4 miles
FRIDAY	Rest Day	
WEEKEND WORKOUT	Leisure Ride. (At least 17 miles non-stop.)	Distance: 25 miles

MONDAY
Intermediate Cycling Exercises

1. Warmup Cycle:	"Dangle loose, ride easy."	Distance: 1¼ miles
2. Cyclesthenics:	The Breather	Count: 20 PTs Coastaway
	The Racer	Count: 20 PTs Recovery Coastaway
3. Training Cycle:	Off Saddle	Count: 40 PTs Coastaway
	Off Saddle	Count: 40 PTs Recovery Coastaway
	REPEAT SEQUENCE:	3 TIMES
4. Test Run:	On and Off Saddle	Distance: 2½ miles

TUESDAY
Rest or optional "joyride"   Distance: 4 miles

WEDNESDAY
Intermediate Cycling Exercises

1. Warmup Cycle:	"Dangle loose, ride easy."	Distance: 1¼ miles
2. Cyclesthenics:	[Same as above].	
3. Training Cycle:	On Saddle	Count: 45 PTs Coastaway
	On Saddle	Count: 45 PTs Recovery Coastaway
	REPEAT SEQUENCE:	4 TIMES
4. Test Run:	On and Off Saddle	Distance: 3 miles

THURSDAY
Scheduled "joyride"   Distance: 4½ miles

FRIDAY
Rest Day

WEEKEND WORKOUT
Leisure Ride. (At least 20 miles non-stop.)   Distance: 30 miles

MONDAY
Intermediate Cycling Exercises

1. Warmup Cycle:	"Dangle loose, ride easy."	Distance: 1¼ miles
2. Cyclesthenics:	The Breather	Count: 20 PTs
		Coastaway
	The Racer	Count: 20 PTs
		Recovery Coastaway
	REPEAT SEQUENCE:	2 TIMES
3. Training Cycle:	On Saddle	Count: 45 PTs
		Coastaway
	Off Saddle	Count: 45 PTs
		Recovery Coastaway
	REPEAT SEQUENCE:	3 TIMES
4. Test Run:	On and Off Saddle	Distance: 3 miles

TUESDAY   Rest or optional "joyride"   Distance: 4½ miles

WEDNESDAY
Intermediate Cycling Exercises

1. Warmup Cycle:	"Dangle loose, ride easy."	Distance: 1¼ miles
2. Cyclesthenics:	[Same as above].	
3. Training Cycle:	Off Saddle	Count: 45 PTs
		Coastaway
	Off Saddle	Count: 45 PTs
		Recovery Coastaway
	REPEAT SEQUENCE:	3 TIMES
4. Test Run:	On and Off Saddle	Distance: 3 miles

THURSDAY   Scheduled "joyride"   Distance: 5 miles

FRIDAY   Rest Day

WEEKEND WORKOUT   Leisure Ride. (At least 25 miles non-stop.)   Distance: 35 miles

WHERE DO YOU GO FROM HERE?

The cycle exercise schedule for week six—level II—*is to be continued for three weeks,* at which time its goals will have been attained IF:

(1) The rider's cycling pace peaks at 15 mph for the various exercise routines.

(2) The workout period for week six exercise schedule does not exceed 30 minutes.

(3) The weekend ride of 35 miles can be accomplished non-stop.

(4) The rider's weekly cycling mileage, whether utilitarian, recreational, and/or as cycling fitness exercise is not less than 50 miles.

At this level of accomplishment, the rider is considered capable of cycling activities under Tourism on a Bike, page 83, and Cycle Clubs, page 84.

He or she may decide to maintain this level of proficiency with less formal cycling practice or a continuance of level II cycle exercise schedules.

Those with an interest in further raising their fitness and bicycling proficiency may proceed to level III, advanced cycle exercise schedules.

LEVEL III: THE ADVANCED CYCLING EXERCISE SCHEDULES

* Points of focus: the advanced cyclist's superior powers of endurance and efficient energy utilization.

* The advanced schedules attain a 75+-miles weekly riding peak. The achievement of this goal qualifies the cyclist for the recreational activities under cycling tours and camping and cycle club activities.

* A medium/fast cycling pace will keep the rider within the 17–25 mph range recommended in the performance of level III cycling exercises.

* Level III, "Up the Grade and Over the Hill," page 78, is for the advanced rider of the "hill and dale" variety.

(See page 51, "How
It's Done")

MONDAY
Advanced Cycling Exercises
   1. Warmup Cycle: "Dangle loose, ride easy."   Distance: 1½ miles
   2. Training Cycle: 100 yards
                 and Coastaway   Six times
                 220 yards
                 and Coastaway   Three times
                 440 yards
                 and Coastaway   Two times
   3. Test Run: On Saddle   Distance: 3¼ miles

TUESDAY   Rest Day

WEDNESDAY
Advanced Cycling Exercises
   1. Warmup Cycle: "Dangle loose, ride easy."   Distance: 1½ miles
   2. Training Cycle: 100 yards
                 and Coastaway   Five times
                 220 yards
                 and Coastaway   Four times
                 440 yards
                 and Coastaway   Two times
   3. Test Run: On Saddle   Distance: 3¼ miles

THURSDAY   Rest Day

FRIDAY   Rest Day

**WEEKEND
  WORKOUT**   Leisure and Training Ride.
                 (At least 30 miles non-
                 stop.)   Distance: 40 miles

LEVEL III | **WEEK TWO** | Medium/Fast
(17–25 MPH)

MONDAY
Advanced Cycling Exercises

1. Warmup Cycle:	"Dangle loose, ride easy."	Distance: 1½ miles
2. Training Cycle:	100 yards	
	and Coastaway	Three times
	220 yards	
	and Coastaway	Three times
	440 yards	
	and Coastaway	Three times
3. Test Run:	On Saddle	Distance: 3¼ miles

TUESDAY | Rest Day

WEDNESDAY
Advanced Cycling Exercises

1. Warmup Cycle:	"Dangle loose, ride easy."	Distance: 1¾ miles
2. Training Cycle:	100 yards	
	and Coastaway	Three times
	220 yards	
	and Coastaway	Four times
	440 yards	
	and Coastaway	Three times
3. Test Run:	On Saddle	Distance: 3½ miles

THURSDAY | Rest Day

FRIDAY | Rest Day

WEEKEND WORKOUT | Leisure and Training Ride. (At least 30 miles non-stop.) | Distance: 40 miles

MONDAY
Advanced Cycling Exercises
1. Warmup Cycle: "Dangle loose, ride easy."   Distance: 1¾ miles
2. Training Cycle: 100 yards
                   and Coastaway   Three times
                   220 yards
                   and Coastaway   Three times
                   440 yards
                   and Coastaway   Four times
3. Test Run: On Saddle   Distance: 3½ miles

TUESDAY   Rest Day

WEDNESDAY
Advanced Cycling Exercises
1. Warmup Cycle: "Dangle loose, ride easy."   Distance: 1¾ miles
2. Training Cycle: 100 yards
                   and Coastaway   Two times
                   220 yards
                   and Coastaway   Four times
                   440 yards
                   and Coastaway   Four times
3. Test Run: On Saddle   Distance: 3½ miles

THURSDAY   Rest Day

FRIDAY   Rest Day

**WEEKEND   Leisure and Training Ride.
   WORKOUT**   (At least 35 miles non-
                   stop.)   Distance: 45 miles

MONDAY
Advanced Cycling Exercises
   1. Warmup Cycle: "Dangle loose, ride easy."   Distance: 2 miles
   2. Training Cycle: 220 yards
      and Coastaway   Two times
      440 yards
      and Coastaway   Two times
      880 yards
      and Coastaway   One time
   3. Test Run: On Saddle   Distance: 4 miles

TUESDAY   Rest Day

WEDNESDAY
Advanced Cycling Exercises
   1. Warmup Cycle: "Dangle loose, ride easy."   Distance: 2 miles
   2. Training Cycle: 220 yards
      and Coastaway   Two times
      440 yards
      and Coastaway   Three times
      880 yards
      and Coastaway   One time
   3. Test Run: On Saddle   Distance: 4 miles

THURSDAY   Rest Day

FRIDAY   Rest Day

WEEKEND   Leisure and Training Ride.
WORKOUT   (At least 35 miles non-
   stop.)   Distance: 45 miles

MONDAY
Advanced Cycling Exercises

1. Warmup Cycle:	"Dangle loose, ride easy."	Distance: 2 miles
2. Training Cycle:	220 yards	
	and Coastaway	Four times
	440 yards	
	and Coastaway	Four times
	880 yards	
	and Coastaway	One time
3. Test Run:	On Saddle	Distance: 4 miles

TUESDAY   Rest Day

WEDNESDAY
Advanced Cycling Exercises

1. Warmup Cycle:	"Dangle loose, ride easy."	Distance: 2½ miles
2. Training Cycle:	220 yards	
	and Coastaway	Four times
	440 yards	
	and Coastaway	Two times
	880 yards	
	and Coastaway	Two times
3. Test Run:	On Saddle	Distance: 4½ miles

THURSDAY   Rest Day

FRIDAY   Rest Day

**WEEKEND
WORKOUT**   Leisure and Training Ride.
(At least 40 miles non-
stop.)   Distance: 50 miles

MONDAY
Advanced Cycling Exercises
   1. Warmup Cycle: "Dangle loose, ride easy."   Distance: 2½ miles
   2. Training Cycle: 220 yards
                   and Coastaway   Three times
                   440 yards
                   and Coastaway   Three times
                   880 yards
                   and Coastaway   Two times
   3. Test Run: On Saddle   Distance: 4½ miles

TUESDAY   Rest Day

WEDNESDAY
Advanced Cycling Exercises
   1. Warmup Cycle: "Dangle loose, ride easy."   Distance: 2½ miles
   2. Training Cycle: 220 yards
                   and Coastaway   Three times
                   440 yards
                   and Coastaway   Three times
                   880 yards
                   and Coastaway   Three times
   3. Test Run: On Saddle   Distance: 4½ miles

THURSDAY   Rest Day

FRIDAY   Rest Day

**WEEKEND
  WORKOUT**   Leisure and Training Ride.
                 (At least 40 miles non-
                 stop.)   Distance: 50+ miles

WHERE DO YOU GO FROM HERE?

The cycle exercise schedule for week six—level III—*is to be continued for three weeks,* at which time its goals will have been attained IF:

(1) The rider's cycling pace peaks at 20–25 mph for the various exercise routines.

(2) The workout period for week six exercise schedules does not exceed 30 minutes.

(3) The weekend ride of 50 miles can be accomplished non-stop, and rides up to 75 miles managed with no more than two brief stops.

(4) The rider's weekly cycling mileage, whether utilitarian, recreational and/or as cycling fitness exercises is not less than 75 miles.

At this level of accomplishment, the rider is considered capable of cycling tours and camping, page 85.

He or she may decide to maintain this level of proficiency with less formal cycling practice, cycling activities or a continuance of cycling exercise schedule level III.

Those hardy few interested in developing still higher cycling fitness and proficiency levels may wish to explore cycle racing activities, whether it be with a view toward becoming an active competitor or deriving the benefit of highly professional training methods. See page 95 for reference sources.

BIKEMANSHIP

Pleasurable cycling means safe and trouble-free riding and many of the highpoints for sound bikemanship outlined here are an invaluable contribution toward this objective. These time-tested rules have been furnished by the Bicycle Institute of America as part of their commendable campaign for bicycle safety. *

Bicycle Safety Code

1. Do not carry passengers.
2. Always observe traffic regulations, stop signs.
3. Use hand signals to indicate turning and stopping.
4. Ride single file.
5. Do not ride from between parked cars.
6. Keep to the right side of the road.
7. Keep both hands on the handlebars.
8. Keep brakes in good condition.
9. Have proper equipment for night riding.
10. Do not speed in busy sections.
11. Avoid crowds.
12. Give right-of-way to pedestrians and automobiles.
13. Do not ride when tired or ill.
14. Avoid stunt riding, racing, and zig-zagging in traffic.
15. Do not "hitch" rides.
16. Slow down, look and listen at all intersections and driveways.
17. Make bicycle repairs off the road.
18. Dismount and walk across heavy traffic.

* Pages 94-96 list free publications on safety and other cycling subjects.

19. Make sure bike is in safe operating condition.
20. Always ride carefully.

Bicycle Safety Regulations

1. Equip bicycle with a lamp on the front and red reflector or lamp on the rear.
2. Equip bicycle with horn or bell in proper operating condition.
3. Obey all traffic signals and signs.
4. Park vehicle in a safe place.
5. Stop while passengers are boarding and alighting from a street car.
6. Never carry any persons on the handlebars.
7. Never ride bicycle on sidewalk unless a local ordinance directs otherwise.
8. Ride in a straight line without weaving.
9. Ride at a safe distance from trucks, buses and other vehicles.
10. Carry packages only if your bicycle has a carrying basket or luggage carrier.
11. Cross all streetcar tracks cartiously and as near to right angles as possible.
12. Avoid riding too fast downhill and on slippery or rough roads.
13. Use guard clips on trouser cuffs if the wheel has no chain guard.
14. Wear light-colored clothing at night so that you can be seen.

Mechanical Safety Precautions

1. Keep your bike in perfect running condition; check the brakes and other vital parts frequently.
2. See that moving parts of the bike are clean and properly lubricated.
3. The axle nuts are tight and wheels are easy to turn and properly aligned.

4. The chain is clean, properly lubricated and free for the right amount of tension.
5. Brake is adjusted so that bike can stop within 10 feet at normal speed.
6. Tires are properly inflated.
7. Frame is straight and true.
8. Seat is adjusted to right height.
9. Pedals are tight and in good repair.
10. Handlebars are tight and set to right height.
11. Front and rear wheels are safely mounted.
12. Replace broken spokes promptly.
13. Replace worn handlegrips and cement them on tightly.

UP THE GRADE AND OVER THE HILL

The Level I Rider: He is advised to stay on generally level areas until he builds up his riding skills. Many over-eager novice cyclists with the middleweight, single-speed bike have a tendency to approach upgrades on the basis of sheer physical power, an ill-advised procedure. The lightweight bike equipped with the common three-speed changes is simple to handle but it does require some experience to benefit from the gear changes in hill climbing.

A maximum of about 5 per cent grade is the advised limit for the level I rider. This means that for about every hundred feet, the rider will have to climb five feet in height. The rules to remember in taking such a grade are simple enough: Do not overwork body motion. Remain steady, without wobbling, and keep to a straight-line course. If a grade is short and somewhat steeper, the level I rider can "make the grade" by picking up enough speed *before* the climb.

The Level II Rider: The cycling skills, distances and activities recommended at this level require the ability to take grades and hills of not too formidable aspect in stride. Because the lightweight bike with the gear changes requires 25 per cent to 30 per cent less rider-energy than the single-speed bike, the advantages of this vehicle are obvious. With skill in the handling of the gears, a 10 per cent grade, which is no small chore even as a walk-up, can be managed by the competent level II rider. The same basic riding principles still apply, of course: Steadiness at the wheel, a straight-line course, proper timing in picking up speed before the ascent, and regular, rhythmic pedalling.

Now for the gear-handling: The shift to lower gear, to take

the strain off the rider's muscles, begins *before* the grade starts to lessen his forward speed. The shift back to high gear comes as the ascent is made. The use of the proper gear requires judgment which comes with experience. Hilly country becomes quite taxing for the rider who is not "gear-wise." This is because he attempts to do with his body what his bicycle gearshift is intended to do for him.

If the longer rides of level II are to be fun, practice with the gearshift is in order as a part of the standard cycling exercise schedules. At this level of proficiency, the rider should include a practice grade in his training course.

The Level III Rider: More rugged and adventuresome cycling tours and camping should be attempted only by the "over-hill-and-dale" rider, the one prepared to go up with his cycle where others must tediously dismount and mount with waning strength and enthusiasm for the entire idea of the trip!

Again, the basic cycling principles for grades and hills apply, but the rider of this level of competency will be up to using a bike of a wider range of gear changes. The Derailleur bike has a multi-speed device with five to 15 speed changes! It takes a lot of know-how to get the most out of such a vehicle. Someone who knows this fine bicycle well can cut the learning time short with sound instruction. Gear changes are not handled all the way up or down as in the three-speed bike. The shift should be made more gradually, a smooth step up from one to the next, in keeping with the upgrade's increasing demand. The rhythm of the ride must not be interfered with. Nor should the varying speed be forced. Knowing footwork is essential for the proper timing to assist in a smooth and effective gear change.

The level III rider is advised to practice and master his gear changes until he can anticipate at a glance the climbing strategy required as a hill or steep ascent comes into view.

On the Way Down

Since "up" includes "over" in hill climbing, the cyclewise rider makes certain that he can handle the braking called for. There is always the hazard of skidding in the downhill momentum, especially if turns are required. And the sudden application of braking can unsaddle the rider, pitching him forward unless he learns how to transfer his weight backward in the braking action. The skillful rider limits sudden braking to unavoidable circumstances.

CYCLING DAY TRIPS

If you have progressed as far as the ninth week of level I, then you are ready to begin to reap many additional rewards for your persistence with the cycling exercise schedules. Already you are quite capable of casually wheeling around town, perhaps over to your job and back, pedalling over to the drugstore, a mahjong or bridge group get-together, or to keep a bowling date. But now, your cycling horizon can begin to expand. Once you know you can manage to go 15 miles and have fun all the way, you can begin to check out bike paths, scenic cycling trails. You can pack a lunch and make it a cycle picnic. If there is a wife and family in the picture, by now they have likely been smitten by the lure of cycling from watching you. You can make it a family outing. This is one kind of pastime the youngsters are only too eager to share with their parents. For those in the state of single blessedness, many cycling companions are easily recruited.

It is important, however, at your cycling level, to check out your destination beforehand, and the condition of the bike route. Avoid actively trafficked thoroughfares. Inquire about facilities for rest and comfort. If you are not in the mood for packing a lunch, find out where you can stop for refreshments. The level I cyclist is wise to select a destination which is at about the halfway mark of his total mileage level. Then he can stop, enjoy that part of the day he chooses in whatever form of recreation he chooses, and then turn about and head for home, happy, relaxed, and none the worse for wear.

Sudden changes in weather and temperature can occur during a day-long outing, but with a bit of forethought you can attain the well-founded boyscout ideal and "be prepared." The listing starting on page 86 might be a helpful beginning in locating a local bike path. But of course, with a bit of exploring and inquiry, you can find other suitable routes. As an afterthought, consider the possibilities of using the railroad to get you out away from your usual surroundings. There is no baggage charge for your bicycle. Or you can plan to ride out and use the railroad back.

TOURISM ON A BIKE

The special benefits for the achievement of level II cycling exercise proficiency can introduce a happy new dimension of experience into your life. You are a 35-miler, and this means that you can do beautifully on prolonged trips planned in 10-, 15-, even 20-mile intervals.

Cycling trips, weekend or week-long and even longer, and cycling travel tours can be yours to enjoy. With careful pre-planning, you can stay within the limits of the tightest budget and still have a wonderful time. The American Youth Hostels are stopover havens for vacationing cyclists *of all ages*. They also plan quite extensive cycling tours both in the United States and abroad, both for families and the individual cyclist.

Still, the level II cyclist should begin gradually with such plans and not try to over-reach himself too soon. His cycle trips should be planned so as to be successively more ambitious. *Planning* still remains, as with the level I cyclist, a most necessary precaution to ensure a happy, safe and fully enjoyable trip. Check out routes to be sure they are negotiable by bicycle. Avoid excessively rugged or hilly terrain. Mark off places for rest, refreshment and scenic and landmark look-abouts.

Tourism on a bike, for the level II cyclist, clearly puts the "tourism" up front. The bike riding is to be regarded as a pleasurable (also economic!) means of novel transport for "getting to specific places and seeing particular things." The dyed-in-the-wool cyclist who puts his riding first and considers other details of his trip as incidental, had better refer to the heading "Cycling Tours and Camping," page 85.

CYCLE CLUBS*

You may never have known that cycle clubs exist. Well, such groups of cycle enthusiasts are to be found all across the country. There may be one in your immediate community!

As a level II cyclist, you can consider club activity, especially if you live in a big city and wish to take to the open country. You may wish to contact such a club, find out something of their activities, the level of riding competency required, and so on, for they may differ appreciably. For example, there are cycle racing clubs. If the response to your inquiry sounds interesting, try a day out with them. You will need to learn about group riding. Some clubs have been around for a considerable time and have seasoned cycle veterans in their ranks who take their cycling most seriously. A get-acquainted visit or ride should help you decide whether a particular club is right for *you*. You can always recruit a group of your own from among your immediate friends. As they begin to see you on wheels regularly, watch their interest leap!

* See page 96 for cycle club booklet.

CYCLING TOURS AND CAMPING

Level III riding proficiency is the requirement here. It is for the cyclist who puts his riding first, is eager to pile on mileage, test his mettle over challenging routes, the cyclist who prefers to keep his planning "loose" so that he may take on adventuresome riding encounters. Rugged terrain, hilly country, even mountain passes are within the range of the hardiest of this breed. Stopover places and activities along the way are decidedly secondary. For this reason, many such inveterate cyclists take to camping. Then they can concentrate on the riding. The simplest cabin or tent abode suffices for the "necessary evil" of sleep in order to awaken to a rosy dawn of more cycling.

Naturally, such an outlook can be tempered with more commodius arrangements along the way.

Extended cycling tours through many foreign countries are commonplace among seasoned riders. Cyclists aspiring to this level of proficiency must build up stamina and train for endurance runs. Brute strength is not the criterion. Many women are capable of moving up into this cycling category. Carefully honed skills—getting the most out of the least energy output—are essential—continuous and untiring cycling rhythms, a knowledge of how to put the bike to work to take up a large measure of the muscular effort, the ability to pace oneself and gauge the most efficient outlay of personal physical resources. The level III cycle exercise schedules can serve as an excellent launching pad for the attainment of this riding plateau.

CYCLING HAVENS

ARIZONA

Maricopa County: Eddie M. Brown, Director, Parks and Recreation, Maricopa County, 622 West Tamarisk Avenue, Phoenix, 85041. Proposed system of bike paths.

Mesa: Maurice B. Bateman, Superintendent of Parks and Recreation, P.O. Box 1280, Mesa, 85202. Park drives or roads (2–3 miles, soil cement), hard surfaced area, bicycle racks.

CALIFORNIA

Avalon: C. J. Conrad, City Administrator, City Hall, Box Y–1. Bicycle racks, rental service (concessionaire).

Chico: Johnie W. Bramble, Jr., Park Superintendent, City of Chico Park Department, 5th and Main Streets. Park drives or roads (15 miles, asphalt and gravel).

Citrus Heights: Richard A. Huebler, Superintendent, Citrus Heights Recreation and Park District, 7801 Auburn Boulevard. Bicycle paths (4 miles, turf), bicycle racks.

Fremont: Leonard H. McVicar, Director, Community Recreation Department, 43551 Mission Boulevard, City Hall. Plans for city-wide network of paths.

Fresno: John A. Suhr, Cadet Supervisor, Fresno Recreation Department, 3030 East Harvey. Park drives or roads (5 miles soil cement, dirt), hard-surfaced area.

Newport Beach: Peter G. Covington, Recreation Superintendent, Parks, Beaches, and Recreation Department, 1714 West Balboa Boulevard. Park drives or roads, hard-surfaces area, parade ground, bicycle racks, rental service (50 bikes, concessionaire).

Oakland: Gordon J. Guetzlaff, Executive Director of Programs, Recreation Department, 1520 Oak Street. Family camp mountain roads (asphalt), rental service (30 bikes, department).

86

San Jose: Bob Amyx, Parks and Recreation, Santa Clara County, 70 West Rosa Street. (Velodrome.)

San Luis Obispo: William E. Flory, Superintendent, Parks and Recreation Department, 864 Santa Rosa Street. Bicycle racks.

Santa Monica: Tom Berling, Department Administrative Assistant, Recreation and Parks Department, Main Street. Concrete walk along beach (3 miles, asphalt, concrete).

Simi: Leslie G. Reed, General Manager, Simi Valley Recreation and Park District, 1734 Los Angeles Avenue. Bicycle paths (17 miles, dirt), park drives or roads.

Sunnyvale: Dick Milkovich, Director, Parks and Recreation Department, City Hall. 45,000 square-foot bicycle path maze.

Yosemite National Park: John C. Preston, Superintendent, Yosemite National Park, California. Rental service (500 bikes, concessionaire).

COLORADO

Colorado Springs: E. S. Richter, Director, Parks and Recreation Department, 1400 North Glen. Bicycle paths, park drives or roads.

Sterling: J. B. Quintin, Superintendent of Parks, Box 590, S. Bikeway (1½ miles, asphalt).

CONNECTICUT

New Haven: James E. Coogan, Director, Parks & Recreation, Box 1416. Bicycle paths (10 miles, asphalt, dirt), park drives or roads, hard-surfaced area, bicycle racks.

Windsor: Harold J. Barenz, Director of Recreation, Windsor Recreation Department, Town Hall. Bicycle paths (½ mile, asphalt), park drives or roads, hard-surfaced area, bicycle racks.

DISTRICT OF COLUMBIA

Washington: T. Sutton Jett, Regional Director, National Capital Region, National Park Service, 1100 Ohio Drive S.W., Washington, D.C. 20242. C. & O. Canal tow path (dirt).

FLORIDA

Clearwater: Gary Garritson, Superintendent of Recreation, 413 Drew Street, 33517. Bike paths and park roads (dirt—proposed to surface with oyster shell).

Miami Beach: Mrs. Marion Wood Huey, Assistant Superintendent of Recreation Department, P.O. Box 646. Track, hard-surfaced area, bicycle racks.

Palm Beach: Robert Jones, Superintendent of Parks, 265 Palmo Way. Bicycle paths (5 miles, asphalt, concrete), rental service (200 bikes, concessionaire).

GEORGIA

Decatur: William C. Scearce, Superintendent of Parks and Recreation Department, 231 Sycamore Street. Hard-surfaced area (5 miles), bicycle racks.

Pine Mountain: Fred C. Galle, Director of Horticulture, Callaway Gardens. Park drives or roads, bicycle racks, rental service (50 bikes, department).

ILLINOIS

Barrington: Richard E. Miller, Director Parks and Recreation, Barrington Park District, Lions Drive. Bikeway, bike safety routes or equivalent (2 miles, soil cement, dirt), track, parade ground, temporary course for racing, bicycle racks, bike rodeo.

Chicago: Erwin Weiner, General Superintendent, Chicago Park District, 425 East 14th Boulevard. Bicycle paths or trails (24 miles, asphalt, concrete), bicycle racks.

Decatur: Harold J. Blankenship, Administrative Assistant, Secretary and Treasurer, Decatur Park District, Box 1136. Bicycle racks.

Northbrook: Edward Rudolph, Superintendent of Parks (Velodrome).

River Forest: Arthur L. Janura, General Superintendent, Forest Preserve District, Cook County, 536 North Harlem Avenue. Bicycle paths or trails (6 miles, asphalt, gravel, dirt, turf).

INDIANA

Butlerville: Arthur Clayton, Recreation Director, Muscatatuck State School, Department of Mental Health. Park drives or roads, hard-surfaced area, bicycle racks.

Indianapolis: R. H. Tolzman, Concession Superintendent, Division of State Parks, 616 State Office Building. Park drives or roads, bicycle racks, rental service (concessionaire).

Valparaiso: Harold M. Gentry, Superintendent of Parks and Recreation, Valparaiso Park District, 53 Franklin Street. Park drives or roads, hard-surfaced area (1 mile, asphalt), bicycle racks.

KANSAS

Garden City: Claude Owens, Superintendent, Park and Zoo, City of Garden City, 309 South Seventh Street. Rental service (6 bikes, concessionaire).

MARYLAND

Patapsco State Park: Spencer P. Ellis, Director, Department of

Forests and Parks, State Office Building, Annapolis, 21404. Bicycle paths and park roads (6 miles, asphalt, dirt).

Silver Spring: John P. Hewitt, Director of Parks, Maryland National Capital Park and Planning Commission, 8787 Georgia Avenue. Bicycle paths (5 miles, blue stone dust), park drives or roads, bicycle racks, rental service (50–300 bikes as needed, concessionaire).

MASSACHUSETTS

Boston: Ben Fink, Chief Engineer, Park Department, 20 Somerset Street. Bicycle paths (5 miles, asphalt, concrete).

Gardner: Henry Dernalowicz, Full-time Commissioner, Recreation Department, City Hall, Room 112. Bicycle paths (10 miles, gravel).

Nantucket: Frank Dinsmore, Secretary, Parks and Recreation Commission, 48 Main Street. Bicycle paths, youth hostel, bicycle racks, rental service (600 bikes).

MICHIGAN

Detroit: Maxwell P. Craig, Superintendent of Public Service, Park and Recreation Department, 735 Randolph. Park drives or roads (10 to 15 miles, asphalt), rental service (100 bikes, concessionaire).

Flint: James A. Bruce, Superintendent, Flint Recreation and Park Board, Room 301, City Hall. Park drives or roads (1 mile, dirt), bicycle racks.

Mackinac Island: Carl A. Nordberg, Superindent, Mackinac Island State Park. Rental service (concessionaire, 7 different rental places).

MINNESOTA

Minneapolis: R. H. Johnson, Director of Recreation, Park Board, 325 City Hall. Bicycle paths (25 miles, asphalt), park drives or roads, hard-surfaced area, parade ground, bicycle racks, rental service (25 bikes, concessionaire).

St. Paul: John K. Rutford, Managerial Assistant Park Department, St. Paul Park, Recreation and Public Building, 545 City Hall. Park drives or roads, bicycle racks, rental service (85 bikes, concessionaire).

MISSOURI

Jackson County: William L. Landahl, Director, Jackson County Park Department, Kansas City, 64106. Proposed system of bicycle paths.

Kansas City: Frank Vaydik, Superintendent, Park Department, City Hall. Park drives or roads (asphalt, concrete), hard-surfaced area, bicycle racks.

Seligman: Donald Reed, Superintendent, Roaring River State Park. Bicycle paths or trails, rental service (30 bikes, concessionaire).

St. Louis: Mrs. Edward G. Brungard, Director, Parks, Recreation and Forestry, 5600 Clayton Road in Forest Park. Bicycle track.

University City: Chauncey I. Linhart, Director of Parks, Recreation and Forests, 6801 Delmar. Park drives or roads (asphalt), hard-surfaced area, bicycle racks.

Webster Groves: W. L. Kloppe, Director Special Services, City and School Department, 16 Selma Avenue. Bicycle paths (10 miles, asphalt, gravel, dirt, turf, concrete), bicycle racks.

MONTANA

Missoula: L. R. Jourdonnais, Superintendent, Park-Recreation Department, Drawer 1226. Bicycle paths (2 miles gravel, dirt), bicycle racks.

NEW HAMPSHIRE

North Conway: Kim Perkins, Director of Recreation, North Conway Community Center, Main Street. Bicycle racks, rental service (50 bikes, concessionaire).

NEW JERSEY

Livingston: Joseph B. Sharpless, Director, Department Recreation and Parks, Memorial Park. Park drives or roads (asphalt), bicycle racks.

Wildwood: Charles L. Juliana, Director of Recreation, City of Wildwood Recreation Department, 243 E. Rio Grande Ave. Boardwalk (5 miles), rental service (1000 bikes, concessionaire).

NEW YORK

Long Island: F. J. Sinnott, Jr., Superintendent of Parks, DPW Division of Parks, Nassau County. Bicycle paths (4–5 miles, asphalt), bikeway, temporary course for racing, bicycle racks.

New York: Samuel M. White, Director of Maintenance and Operation, City of New York Department of Parks, 64th Street and 5th Avenue, New York. Bicycle paths (50 miles, asphalt, concrete), track.

Port Washington: Alfred L. Whitney, Supervisor of H.P.E. & R., Port Washington Public Schools, Main Street. Bicycle racks.

Salamanca: Leigh J. Batterson, Regional Park Manager, Allegany State Park Commission, Allegany State Park. Park drives or roads, rental service (30 bikes, concessionaire).

White Plains: Joseph E. Curtis, Commissioner, Recreation and Parks

Department, Gedney Way. Bikeway, temporary course for racing, bicycle racks.

NORTH CAROLINA

Clinton: B. Hunter Wells, Director of Recreation, Fisher Drive. Bicycle paths (2 miles, dirt, turf), temporary course for racing, bicycle racks.

OHIO

Cleveland: Harold W. Groth, Director, Cleveland Metropolitan Park District, 2049 Standard Building, Cleveland 13, Ohio. Bicycle route (10 miles, asphalt).

Columbus: William F. Walton, Parks Assistant Superintendent, Division Parks & Forestry, 1826 Franklin Park South. Park drives or roads (2 miles, asphalt, gravel, concrete), temporary course for racing, bicycle racks.

Dayton: Kettering: John Somers, Superintendent Parks and Recreation, Municipal Building, 101 West Third Street. Bicycle route in Montgomery County.

Deer Park: William Smith, Park Superintendent, Recreation Department, City Hall, Matson & Blue Ash Roads. Bicycle paths (asphalt), bikeway, hard-surfaced area, bicycle racks.

Hamilton: James W. Grimm, Superintendent of Recreation, City-School Recreation Department, Board of Education Building. Bicycle paths or trails, youth hostel.

PENNSYLVANIA

Abington: James C. Dittmar, Superintendent, Parks and Recreation Department, 1176 Old York Road. Bicycle paths (2½ miles, asphalt), bicycle racks, rental service (100 bikes, department).

Harrisburg: Robert E. Sutherland, Director of Recreation, Bureau of Recreation, Reservoir Park. Bicycle paths (8 miles, asphalt, concrete), park drives or roads, hard-surfaced area, bicycle racks, rental service (28 miles, department).

Philadelphia: Harold Schick, Director, Fairmount Park Commission, Belmont, West Fairmount Park. Bikeway, park drives or roads (20 miles, asphalt, concrete), hard-surfaced area, youth hostel, temporary course for racing, bicycle racks.

SOUTH DAKOTA

Mitchell: Joe L. Collins, Superintendent of Parks, City Parks Department, City Building. Bicycle paths (1-2-3 miles, gravel), park drives or roads, hard-surfaced area, bicycle racks.

TEXAS

Abilene: Terry O'Brien, Recreation Superintendent, Parks & Recreation Department, Box 60, City Hall. Bicycle racks.

Austin: Warren G. Leddick, Assistant Director, Parks and Recreation Department, 1500 West Riverside Drive. Bicycle paths or trails.

Corpus Christi: Ken Krenek, Park Superintendent, Box 1622. Bicycle racks.

Crystal City: George Ozuna, Jr., City Manager, Parks Department. Bikeway (1½ miles, asphalt, concrete), temporary course for racing.

Dallas: L. B. Houston, Director, Parks and Recreation Department, 506 Municipal Building. Park drives or roads, hard-surfaced area, bicycle racks, rental service (50 bikes, concessionaire).

Edinburg: John Economedes, Director, Parks and Recreation, P.O. Drawer 1079. Bicycle paths (3 miles, asphalt, gravel, concrete), Bikeway, track, park drives or roads, hard-surfaced area, parade ground, bicycle racks.

Waco: Alva Stem, Director, Parks and Recreation Department, 300 Bridle Path Road. P.O. Box 1370. Park drives or roads (10 miles, asphalt, gravel, concrete), hard-surfaced area, bicycle racks.

VIRGINIA

Martinsville: William H. Smith, Director of Recreation, Recreation Department, Cleveland Avenue. Bicycle paths (5 miles, gravel), hard-surfaced area, bicycle racks.

WASHINGTON

Seattle: Les Maynock, Administrative Assistant, Seattle Park Department, 100 Dexter Avenue, North. Bicycle paths or trails (3 miles, crushed rock, compacted), bicycle racks.

WISCONSIN

Fond du Lac: W. LaBorde, Recreation Director, Public Recreation Department, 109 E. Merrill Street. Temporary course for racing, bicycle racks.

Janesville: Pat Dawson, Recreation Director, c/o Marshall Junior High School, 408 South Main Street. Hard-surfaced area, bicycle racks.

Kenosha: Eugene Hammond, Mayor. (Velodrome.)

Milwaukee: Howard W. Gregg, General Manager, Milwaukee County Park Commission, 308 Court House. Track, Bikeways (64 miles, asphalt), park drives or roads, bicycle racks.

Oshkosh: John R. Torrini, Superintendent of Parks and City Forester, Service Department, City Hall. Bicycle paths, park drives or roads, hard-surfaced area, rental service (20 bikes, concessionaire).

Watertown: James J. Niles, Director, Department of Recreation, City Hall. Bicycle racks, rental service (8 bikes, concessionaire).

TOURING INFORMATION

Write to:

AMERICAN YOUTH HOSTELS, INC.
   20 West 17th Street
   New York, New York

   Promotes low-cost vacation trips by bike

BICYCLE TOURING LEAGUE OF AMERICA
   Roland C. Geist
   260 West 26th Street
   New York, New York

   Provides cycle touring information

INTERNATIONAL BICYCLE TOURING SOCIETY
   Dr. Clifford Graves
   846 Prospect Street
   La Jolla, California

   Promotes extended bicycle trips for experienced cyclists,
   home and abroad

LEAGUE OF AMERICAN WHEELMEN
   Mrs. Joseph L. Hart, Secretary
   5118 Foster Avenue
   Chicago, Illniois

   National organization of adult recreational cyclists.

RACING INFORMATION

Write to:

AMATEUR BICYCLE LEAGUE OF AMERICA
Alfred Toefield, President
87-66 256th Street
Floral Park, Long Island, New York

This is the governing body of competitive cycling in America.

CANADIAN WHEELMENS ASSOCIATION
Paul Suave Center
4000 Beaubien Street East
Montreal, P.Q., Canada

The governing body of competitive cycling in Canada.

EASTERN CYCLING FEDERATION
Frank Small
4233 205th Street
Bayside, New York

EASTERN INTERCOLLEGIATE CYCLING ASSOCIATION
August Husse
95 East Deshler Avenue
Columbus, Ohio

A division of ABLA, governs all college-level bike racing.

PUBLICATIONS

Free Publications of the Bicycle Institute of America:
    122 East 42nd Street
    New York, New York 10017

BICYCLE RIDING CLUBS
BIKE RACING ON CAMPUS
BIKE REGULATIONS IN THE COMMUNITY
BIKE FUN
BICYCLE SAFETY SET
BIKEWAYS

American Association for Health, Physical Education and Recreation:
    1201 Sixteenth Street, N.W.
    Washington 36, D.C.

CYCLING IN THE SCHOOL FITNESS PROGRAM ($1.00)

The Huffman Manufacturing Company:
    Dayton 1, Ohio
A HANDBOOK ON BICYCLE TRACKS AND CYCLE RACING
(Free)